Oh Baby,

I'm Having a Baby!

Wise, Witty, Warm, and Wildly Wry Quotes

for the Mother-To-Be

by: Torran Bagamary and Michelle Iglesias

CCC Books
PO Box 1827
Westfield, MA 01086

by: Torran Bagamary and Michelle Iglesias

Copyright © 2008 CCC Books

All rights reserved

Published in the U.S.A. by CCC Books

PO Box 1827, Westfield, MA 01086

(413) 214-4770

stores.lulu.com/cccbooks

ISBN # 978-0-6152-0874-9

*In memory of Michael B. Lynn
and his three loving dogs,
Chewy, Chuck and Cheese*

Table of Contents

On Being Pregnant	pg. 7
On Giving Birth	pg. 33
On Having a Newborn	pg. 63
On Being a Mom	pg. 113
Index	pg. 142

ON BEING PREGNANT

Being pregnant can be one of the most wondrous and magical adventures that you can ever experience. You will most likely feel love, patience and other emotions that bubble up within you.

Anonymous

Your baby will only be in you for nine months, so enjoy the intimacy as long as it lasts.

Anonymous

A mother's joy begins

when new life is stirring inside…

when a tiny heartbeat is heard for the very first time,

and a playful kick reminds her that

she is never alone.

Anonymous

You also look forward to your baby's arrival

in this world with huge anticipation.

You long for the day when you can finally

physically carry your baby in your arms

and look at your baby in the eyes.

Anonymous

Knowing you are going to have a child

is like extending yourself in the world,

setting up a tent and saying,

"Here I am, I am important."

Now that I'm going to have a child

it's like the balance is even. My hand is as rich as

theirs, maybe for the first time.

I am no longer just a child.

Anonymous

Pregnancy is 40 weeks at term.

Your baby will NEVER be easier to take care of

than it is right there inside of you.

Don't rush it!

Anonymous

I think that carrying a baby inside of you

is like running as fast as you can.

It feels like finally letting go

and filling yourself up to the widest limits.

Anonymous

Love and pregnancy and riding on a camel

cannot be hid.

Arabic Proverb

Think of stretch marks

as pregnancy service stripes.

Joyce Armor

You should never say anything to a woman

that even remotely suggests

that you think she's pregnant

unless you can see an actual baby

emerging from her at that moment.

Dave Barry

When I had reached my term,

I looked like a rat dragging a stolen egg.

Sidonie Gabrielle Colette

By far the most common craving of pregnant women

is not to be pregnant.

Phyllis Diller

It would seem that something which means

poverty, disorder and violence every single day

should be avoided entirely,

but the desire to beget children is a natural urge.

Phyllis Diller

If men were equally at risk from this condition –
if they knew their bellies might swell as if
they were suffering from end-stage cirrhosis,
that they would have to go nearly a year
without a stiff drink, a cigarette, or even an aspirin,
that they would be subject to fainting spells
and unable to fight their way onto commuter trains —
then I am sure that pregnancy would be classified as
a sexually transmitted disease and abortions would
be no more controversial than
emergency appendectomies.

Barbara Ehrenreich

You do a lot of growing up when you're pregnant.

It's suddenly like,

"Yikes. Here it is folks. Playtime is over."

Connie Fioretto

Everything grows rounder and wider and weirder,

and I sit here in the middle of it all and wonder

who in the world you will turn out to be.

Carrie Fisher

Meredith: I think we ought to get married.

We don't fight, we love it in bed,

and – well, that's about it, really.

Jos: You must be pregnant.

Meredith: Yes.

Margaret Forster

A ship under sail and a big-bellied woman,

Are the handsomest two things

that can be seen common.

Benjamin Franklin

Every four weeks I go up a braw size…

it's worth being pregnant just for the breast.

Natasha Hamilton

What's that on the telly?

It's an angel sent from God…

Growing in my belly…

Like a sweet pea in a pod!

Melissa Hatcher

Oh, what a tangled web we weave

when first we practice to conceive.

Don Herold

I got so much advice; I just started tuning it out.

If one more person told me what I had to do

when the baby comes, I was going to shoot'em.

Kate Hudson

Being slightly paranoid

is like being slightly pregnant—

it tends to get worse.

Molly Ivins

Whether our pregnancy was meticulously planned,

medically coaxed, or happened by surprise,

one thing is certain –

your life will never be the same.

Catherine Jones

If men could get pregnant,

abortion would be a sacrament.

Florence R. Kennedy

Pregnancy represents one of the

greatest unknowns in life.

Everyone's at least a little worried about

how it will turn out.

Lawrence Kutner

Pregnancy is a disease

from which you recover

in 18 years and 9 months.

Carrie Latet

I didn't know how babies were made

until I was pregnant with my fourth child.

Loretta Lynn

The breasts go first,

and then the waist, and then the butt.

Nobody ever tells you that you get

a butt when you get pregnant.

Elle MacPherson

The only time a woman wishes she was

a year older is when she's

expecting a baby.

Mary Marsh

No matter how much you wish for privacy,

your pregnancy is a public event

to which everyone feels invited.

Jean Marzollo

We can see the child moving

rather serenely in the uterus.

The child senses aggression in its sanctuary.

We see the child's mouth wide open

in a silent scream.

Dr. Bernard Nathanson

Everything about women is a riddle,

and everything about women has a single solution:

that is, pregnancy.

Friedrich Nietzsche

I got a really big baby

growing out of my stomach and,

quite frankly, it looks like

I've I got one growing out of my bottom, too.

Fay Ripley

In the pregnancy process I have come to realize

how much of the burden is on the female partner.

She's got a construction zone going on in her belly.

Al Roker

When sperm and egg unite,

something goes from inanimate to animate.

It is life.

Mitt Romney

How can I have morning sickness

when I don't get up till noon?

Rita Rudner

Life is tough enough without having someone

kick you from the inside.

Rita Rudner

They're trying to put warning labels on liquor saying, "Caution, alcohol can be dangerous to pregnant women." That's ironic. If it weren't for alcohol, most women wouldn't even be that way.

Rita Rudner

After my first pregnancy,

all of my fat went to my thighs.

All of my husband's fat went to his head.

Molly Ryan

My body knows just what to do.

My baby grows just as it should be.

Penny Sikin

In the creative process there is

the father, the author of the play;

the mother, the actor pregnant with the part,

and the child, the role to be born.

Constantine Stanislavsky

Her girlfriends asked that innocent,

"What? What appeals to you?"

when her pregnancy cravings appeared.

Her gaze merely fell on her husband.

Hla Stavhana

Pregnancy is a kind of miracle.

Especially in that it proves that

a man and woman can conspire

to force God to create a new soul.

Robert Anton Wilson

I begin to love this creature,

And to anticipate her birth

As a fresh twist to a knot,

Which I do not wish to untie.

Mary Wollstonecraft

ON GIVING BIRTH

The moment you hold your baby

in your arms for the first time,

you wonder how could such a tiny bundle of thing

create so much emotions within you.

And you wonder if it's possible that you've actually

brought such a tiny, beautiful being into this world.

Anonymous

The power and intensity of your contractions

cannot be stronger than you,

because it IS YOU.

Anonymous

Anyone who thinks women are the weaker sex never witnessed childbirth.

Anonymous

It is somehow reassuring to discover that the word "travel" is derived from "travail", denoting the pains of childbirth.

Anonymous

Babies fill a hole in your heart

that you never knew existed.

Anonymous

Prepared childbirth is a contradiction in terms.

Joyce Armor

The knowledge of how to give birth without outside interventions lies deep within each woman. Successful childbirth depends on the acceptance of the process.

Suzanne Arms

Baby's room should be close enough to your room

so that you can hear baby cry,

unless you want to get some sleep,

in which case baby's room should be in Peru.

Dave Barry

If a woman has to choose between

catching a fly ball and saving an infant's life,

she will choose to save the infant's life

without even considering if there are men on base.

Dave Barry

The old system of having a baby

was much better than the new system,

the old system being characterized by the fact

that the men didn't have to watch.

Dave Barry

Childbirth, as a strictly physical phenomenon,

is comparable to driving a United Parcel truck

through an inner tube.

Dave Barry

Every Night and every Morn

Some to Misery are born.

Every Morn and every Night

Some are born to Sweet Delight,

Some are born to Endless Night.

William Blake

Our Lamaze instructor… assured our class… that our cervix muscles would become "naturally numb" as they swelled and stretched, and deep breathing would turn the final explosions of pain into "manageable discomfort". This description turned out to be as accurate as, say a steward advising passengers aboard the Titanic to prepare for a brisk but bracing swim.

Mary Kay Blakely

They say a man can never

experience the pain of childbirth.

They can…if you hit them in the goolies

with a cricket bat for fourteen hours.

Jo Brand

The parallels between making love and giving birth

are clear, not only in terms of passion and love,

but also because we need essentially

the same conditions for both experiences:

privacy and safety.

Sarah Buckley

Having a baby is like

taking your bottom lip

and pulling it over your head.

Carol Burnett

Just how a women's heart knows

how and when to pump, her lungs when to inhale,

and her hand to pull back from fire,

so she knows when and how to give birth.

Virginia Di Orio

Many women have described their experiences of childbirth as being associated with a spiritual uplifting, the power of which they have never previously been aware... To such a woman childbirth is a monument of joy within her memory. She turns to it in thought to seek again an ecstasy, which passed too soon.

Grantly Dick-Read

Heaven grant that the burden you carry may have as easy an exit as it had an entrance.

Erasmus

Childbirth classes neglect to teach one critical skill:

How to breath, count, and swear

all at the same time.

Linda Filterman

God's interest in the human race

is nowhere better evinced than in obstetrics.

Martin H. Fischer

ON GIVING BIRTH

Watching a baby being born

is a little like watching a wet St. Bernard

coming in through the cat door.

Jeff Foxworthy

When I first came out from under the anesthesia

and opened my eyes to see my baby,

my heart filled with love and thanks to God for

sending her to me. How can I express how I felt

the first time I held her

and her blue eyes gazed up into mine?

How can you describe a miracle?

Annette Funicello

I was awake for the whole unbelievable birth.

It was so emotional I sobbed through the entire

experience...And then I saw the doctor lift him up.

It is the single most amazing experience

a human being could ever have.

Kathie Lee Gifford

I realize why women die in childbirth—

it's preferable.

Sherry Glaser

It's funny, to me, the way people

refer to childbirth as a miraculous event.

A miracle is something that defies nature.

Only, childbirth has got to be the most

natural thing in the world. Top three anyway.

But, on the other hand, when you think about it,

there's really no other word that fits.

Sperm. Egg. A Coincidental meshing of genetic

information that will grow something that could

write an opera or cook up some Napalm.

It blows my mind.

Barbara Hall

We have a secret in our culture,

and it's not that birth is painful.

It's that women are strong.

Laura Stavoe Harm

Birth is as safe as life gets.

Harriette Hartigan

Childbirth is no more a miracle

then eating food and a turd coming out of your ass.

Bill Hicks

My husband was just OK looking.

I was in labor and said to him,

"What if she's ugly? You're ugly."

Beverly Johnson

There's an African story of birth where the women

gather and send you across the river,

and as you walk across this log across the river

you head out with these women.

As you go across on the narrowest part you're alone.

No one can be there with you, and as you emerge

onto the other side of the river,

all the women who have given birth

are there to greet you.

Liz Koch

Birth is an experience that demonstrates that life

is not merely function and utility,

but form and beauty.

Christopher Largen

Birthing is the most profound initiation to spirituality

a woman can have.

Robin Lim

A healthy woman who delivers spontaneously performs a job that cannot be improved upon.

Aidan MacFarlane

In the best of all possible worlds,

childbirth enriches a marriage.

In the worst, it harms it.

No matter how good their marriage is,

most couples find that having a baby

challenges their relationship.

Jean Marzollo

Because they've either conveniently forgotten with time or they're trying to be supportive, most mothers won't tell you how hard pregnancy (and then childbirth) can be. Let me tell you, it is. It's brutal sometimes! But, if I did it, ANYONE can do it.

I mean, I always knew I was meant to do something really BIG in life, and now I know that this was it. Screw winning an Academy Award someday...

I GAVE BIRTH!

Jenny McCarthy

The whole point of women-centered birth

is the knowledge that a woman is the birth power

source. She may need, and deserve, help,

but in essence, she always had, currently has,

and will have the power.

Heather McCue

To enter life by way of the vagina

is as good a way as any.

Henry Miller

Death and taxes and childbirth!

There's never any convenient time for any of them.

Margaret Mitchell

I have personally come to believe that childbirth

is a blessing to women sent straight from God.

I mean, in its purest form, birth is

the most fantastic orgasm married with a miracle!

What more heavenly gift could there be?

Laurie Annis Morgan

I once heard two ladies going on and on about the pains of childbirth and how men don't seem to know what pain really is. I asked if either of them have ever got themselves caught in a zipper.

Emo Philips

I'd be happy to stand next to any man I know in one of those labor rooms the size of a Volkswagen and whisper, "No dear, you don't really need the Demerol; just relax and do your second stage breathing."

Anna Quindlen

ON GIVING BIRTH

I think, at a child's birth,

if a mother could ask a fairy godmother to

endow it with the most useful gift,

that gift would be curiosity.

Eleanor Roosevelt

The same movements that get the baby in,

get the baby out.

Eleanor Roosevelt

Birth is not only about making babies.

Birth is about making mothers…

strong, competent, capable mothers

who trust themselves and know their inner strength.

Barbara Katz Rothman

Childbirth is more admirable than conquest,

more amazing than self-defense,

and as courageous as either one.

Gloria Steinem

"Delivery" is the wrong word to describe

the childbearing process.

Delivery is: "Here's your pizza."

Takes 30 minutes or less.

"Exorcism", I think, is more apt:

"Please, get the hell out of my body!"

Jeff Stilson

Childbirth is a time when a woman's power and strength emerge full force, but it is also a vulnerable time, and a time of many changes presenting opportunities for personal growth.

Anne Marie Van Oploo

Childbirth provided the drama I craved, the thrill of peeking over the primal edge of creation, the rush of the unexpected.

Peggy Vincent

Women's bodies have

near-perfect knowledge of childbirth;

it's when their brains get involved

that things can go wrong.

Peggy Vincent

Giving birth should be your greatest achievement

not your greatest fear.

Jane Weideman

ON HAVING A NEWBORN

A baby is sunshine and moonbeams

and more brightening your world as never before.

Anonymous

Ten fingers, Ten toes

She's laughter and teardrops

So small and brand new

And amazing angelic

She's sent to bless you

She's one special Baby

The best of life's treasure

And will grant and bless you

Many hours of great pleasure.

Anonymous

Ten tiny fingers that always want to play,

That never stop exploring the wonder of today.

Ten tiny little fingers that from the very start,

Will reach out for tomorrow

yet always hold your heart.

Anonymous

When they placed you in my arms,

you slipped into my heart.

Anonymous

Having a baby is one of the most

magical moments of your life.

It practically turns your world upside down.

Anonymous

The joy of having a baby today

can only be described in two words:

tax deduction.

Anonymous

A baby usually wakes up

in the wee-wee hours of the morning.

Anonymous

A baby will make love stronger, days shorter,

nights longer, bankroll smaller, home happier,

clothes shabbier, the past forgotten,

and the future worth living for.

Anonymous

Child rearing myth #1:

Labor ends when the baby is born.

Anonymous

A baby is an angel

whose wings decrease as his legs increase.

Anonymous

ON HAVING A NEWBORN

If you were to open up a baby's head—

and I'm not for a moment

suggesting that you should—

you would find nothing

but an enormous drool gland.

Dave Barry

There are two things in life for which

we are never truly prepared:

twins.

Josh Billings

I don't know any parents that look into

the eyes of a newborn baby and say,

"How can we screw this kid up?"

Russell Bishop

If your baby is beautiful and perfect,

never cries or fusses, sleeps on schedule

and burps on demand, an angel all the time,

you're the grandma.

Theresa Bloomingdale

Attachment to a baby is a long-term process,

not a single, magical moment.

The opportunity for bonding at birth

may be compared to falling in love—

staying in love takes longer

and demands more work.

T. Berry Brazelton

Having a baby changes the way

you view your in-laws.

I love it when they come to visit now.

They can hold the baby and I can go out.

Matthew Broderick

Except that right side up is best,

there is not much to learn about holding a baby.

There are one hundred and fifty-two distinctly

different ways—and all are right!

At least all will do.

Heywood Broun

Having a baby is like falling in love again,

both with your husband and your child.

Tina Brown

People who say they sleep like a baby

usually don't have one.

Leo J. Burke

There are three reasons for breast-feeding;

the milk is always at the right temperature;

it comes in attractive containers;

and the cat can't get it.

Irena Chalmers

Every child born has innate goodness.

Chinese Proverb

It is the nature of babies to be in bliss.

Deepak Chopra

A baby is born with a need to be loved

and never outgrows it.

Frank Clark

A child, like your stomach,

doesn't need all you can afford to give it.

Frank Clark

Having a child is surely

the most beautifully irrational act

that two people in love can commit.

Bill Cosby

Babies are unreasonable;

they expect far too much of existence.

Each new generation that comes

takes one look at the world, thinks wildly,

"Is *this* all they've done to it?" and bursts into tears.

Clarence Day

Every baby born into this world

is a finer one than the last.

Charles Dickens

Language was not powerful enough

to describe the infant phenomenon.

Charles Dickens

Babies are beautiful, wonderful, exciting, enchanting, extraordinary little creatures—who grow up into ordinary folk like us.

Doris Dyson

Infancy conforms to nobody; all conform to it, so that one babe commonly makes four or five out of the adults who prattle and play to it.

Ralph Waldo Emerson

ON HAVING A NEWBORN

When you have a baby, you set off an explosion in your marriage, and when the dust settles, your marriage is different from what it was. Not better, necessarily; not worse, necessarily; but different.

Nora Ephron

Everyone knows that by far the happiest and universally enjoyable age of man is the first. What is there about babies which makes us hug and kiss and fondle them, so that even an enemy would give them help at that age?"

Desiderius Erasmus

Babies control and bring up their families as much as they are controlled by them; in fact…

the family brings up baby

by being brought up by him.

Erik H. Erikson

Insomnia: A contagious disease

often transmitted from babies to parents.

Shannon Fife

When a child enters the world through you,

it alters everything on a psychic,

psychological and purely practical level.

You're just not free anymore to do

what you want to do.

And it's not the same again.

Ever.

Jane Fonda

When babies look beyond you and giggle,

maybe they're seeing angels.

Eileen Elias Freeman

I don't know why they say "you have a baby".

The baby has you.

Robert Gallagher

It doesn't matter how many books you read before your baby arrives; nothing gets you ready for that first night when you're out of the hospital and alone, and she's crying and won't stop, and your holding her against you while her screams rock your chest.

Bob Greene

Breastfeeding should not be attempted

by fathers with hairy chests,

since they can make the

baby sneeze and give it wind.

Mike Harding

Babies are such a nice way to start people.

Don Herold

Babies haven't any hair;

Old men's heads are just as bare;

Between the cradle and the grave

Lies a haircut and a shave.

Samuel Hoffenstein

Families with babies and families without babies

are sorry for each other.

Ed Howe

The worst feature of a new baby

is its mother's singing.

Kin Hubbard

If you desire to drain to the dregs

the fullest cup of scorn and hatred

that a fellow human being can pour out for you,

let a young mother hear you

call dear baby "it."

Jerome K Jerome

This baby is a miracle.

It's like God nodding and saying,

"I'm pleased with what you've done."

Ann Jillian

A baby changes your dinner party conversation

from politics to poops.

Maurice Johnstone

For any normal woman in normal circumstances

there is bound to be a special excitement and joy

and gratitude to God when she

holds her first baby in her arms.

Rose Fitzgerald Kennedy

Now the thing about having a baby—

and I can't be the first person to have noticed this—

is that thereafter you have it.

Jean Kerr

For success in training children

the first condition is to become as a child oneself,

but this means no assumed childishness,

no condescending baby-talk . . .

What it does mean is to be taken up with the child

as the child himself is absorbed by his life.

Ellen Key

Miracles DO happen…

Love him like heaven begins tomorrow.

Peggy Kubic

It's so easy during those first few months

to think that the problems will never end.

You feel as if your son

will never sleep through the night,

will always spit up food after eating,

and will never learn to smile—

even though you don't know any adults

or even older children who still act this way.

Lawrence Kutner

Babies Leak.

From both ends.

Bruce Lansky

A new baby is like the beginning of all things—

wonder, hope, a dream of possibilities.

Eda J. Le Shan

Loving a baby is a circular business,

a kind of feedback loop.

The more you give the more you get

and the more you get

the more you feel like giving.

Penelope Leach

No animal is so inexhaustible

as an excited infant.

Amy Leslie

Where did you come from, baby dear?

Out of the everywhere and into here.

George MacDonald

A Baby is something you carry

inside you for nine months,

in your arms for three years

and in your heart till the day you die.

Mary Manson

One of the most important

things to remember about infant care is:

never change the diapers in midstream.

Don Marquis

Babies are competent individuals

who should have their own agenda

and should be treated with respect.

Ruth Mason

Diaper backward spells repaid.

Think about it.

Marshall McLuhan

A woman can learn a lot from holding a new baby.

It is life beginning again—sweet possibilities!

No problem in the world

is big enough to be remembered.

Susan McOmber

The only language men ever speak perfectly

is the one they learn in babyhood,

when no one can teach them anything!

Maria Montessori

In early infancy, the baby tends to experience

herself and her mother as one, a union.

If the mother responds attentively and

empathetically to the infant, a life-sustaining function

is provided which is felt to be part of the baby's self.

Andrew P. Morrison

A bit of talcum

Is always walcum.

Ogden Nash

Of all the joys that lighten suffering earth,

what joy is welcomed like a newborn child?

Dorothy L. Nolte

You fall in love, instantly.

I thought he was the most beautiful boy

I had ever seen.

Rosie O'Donnell

I always wondered why babies

spend so much time sucking their thumbs.

Then I tasted baby food.

Robert Orben

Babies are always more trouble than you thought—

and more wonderful.

Charles Osgood

Did you ever notice that a new baby

always seems to bear a striking resemblance

to the relative who has the most money?

Robert Paul

Anyone who has breast-fed

knows two things for sure:

The baby wants to be fed

at the most inopportune times,

in the most inopportune places,

and the baby will prevail...

And so the baby should, and the mom, too.

Sometimes a breast is a sexual object,

and sometimes it's a food delivery system,

and one need not preclude nor color the other.

Anna Quindlen

A baby is an alimentary canal

with a loud voice at one end

and no responsibility at the other.

Ronald Reagan

People often ask me, "What's the difference

between couplehood and babyhood?"

In a word. Moisture.

Everything in my life is now more moist.

Between your spittle, your diapers,

your spit-up and drool, you got your baby food,

your wipes, your formula, your leaky bottles,

sweaty baby backs, and numerous

other untraceable sources—

all creating an ever-present moistness in my life,

which heretofore was mainly dry.

Paul Reiser

Every baby needs a lap.

Henry Robin

I once knew a chap who had a system of just hanging the baby on the clothesline to dry and he was greatly admired by his fellow citizens for having discovered a wonderful innovation on changing a diaper.

Damon Runyon

ON HAVING A NEWBORN

A baby is God's opinion that the world should go on.

Carl Sandburg

Don't forget that compared to a grownup person

every baby is a genius. Think of the capacity to learn!

The freshness, the temperament,

the will of a baby a few months old!

May Sarton

Babies need social interactions with loving adults

who talk with them, listen to their babblings,

name objects for them,

and give them opportunities

to explore their worlds.

Sandra Scarr

A baby is a blank check

made payable to the human race.

Barbara Christine Seifert

ON HAVING A NEWBORN

Child, the current of your breath

is six days long.

You lie, a small knuckle on my white bed;

lie, fisted like a snail,

so small and strong at my breast.

Your lips are animals;

you are fed with love.

Anne Sexton

The smell of his silky head,

the clutch of minuscule fingers

against my breast as he nursed.

Cleaning him, caring for him,

dressing him in soft cottons—

doing a good job with my baby

brought me free-floating joy.

Linda Gray Sexton

You can sort of be married,

you can sort of be divorced,

you can sort of be living together,

but you can't sort of have a baby.

David Shire

It sometimes happens,

even in the best of families, that a baby is born.

This is not necessarily cause for alarm.

The important thing is to keep your wits about you

and borrow some money.

Elinor Goulding Smith

A wee bit of heaven

Drifted down from above

A handful of happiness

A heartful of love

A mystery of life

So sacred and so sweet

The giver of joy

So deep and complete.

Precious and priceless

So lovable too

The world's sweetest miracle

Baby, it's you.

Helen Steiner-Rice

A babe in the house is a well-spring of pleasure,

a messenger of peace and love,

a resting place for innocence on earth,

a link between angels and men.

Martin Fraquhar Tupper

Adam and Eve had many advantages,

but the principal one was that they escaped teething.

Mark Twain

If one feels the need of something grand,

something infinite, something that makes one feel

aware of God, one need not go far to find it.

I think that I see something deeper, more infinite,

more eternal than the ocean in the expression of the

eyes of a little baby when it wakes in the morning

and coos or laughs because

it sees the sun shining on its cradle.

Vincent Van Gogh

If you want a baby, have a new one.

Don't baby the old one.

Jessamyn West

Every child born into the world

is a new thought of God,

an ever fresh and radiant possibility.

Kate Douglas Wiggin

Mark the babe not long accustomed

to this breathing world;

One that hath barely learned to shape a smile,

though yet irrational of soul,

to grasp with tiny finger—to let fall a tear;

And, as the heavy cloud of sleep dissolves,

To stretch his limbs, becoming, as might seem.

The outward functions of intelligent man.

William Wordsworth

ON BEING A MOM

This is the reason why mothers are more devoted

to their children than fathers:

it is that they suffer more in giving them birth

and are more certain that they are their own.

Aristotle

What the mother sings to the cradle

goes all the way down to the coffin.

Francis Bacon

We never know the love of the parent

till we become parents ourselves.

Henry Ward Beecher

Most of us would do more for our babies

than we have ever been willing to do for anyone,

even ourselves.

Polly Berrien Berends

Parenthood always comes as a shock.

Postpartum blues? Postpartum panic is more like it.

We set out to have a baby;

what we get is a total take-over of our lives.

Polly Berrien Berends

We can see that the baby is

as much an instrument of nourishment for us

as we are for him.

Polly Berrien Berends

If evolution really works,

how come mothers only have two hands?

Milton Berle

When a woman is twenty, a child deforms her;

when she is thirty, he preserves her;

and when forty, he makes her young again.

Leon Blum

Your children will become what you are;

so be what you want them to be.

David Bly

It is not until you become a mother

that your judgment slowly turns to

compassion and understanding.

Erma Bombeck

I was a mother.

I wanted to laugh.

I felt such pride,

such an incredible sense of wholeness.

Diahann Carroll

A mother understands what a child does not say.

Chinese proverb

There is only one pretty child in the world,

and every mother has it.

Chinese Proverb

To understand your parents' love

you must raise children yourself.

Chinese proverb

Feeling fat lasts nine months

but the joy of becoming a mom lasts forever.

Nikki Dalton

You should study not only that you

become a mother when your child is born,

but also that you become a child.

Dogen

While everything else in our lives

has gotten simpler, speedier,

more microwavable and user-friendly,

child-raising seems to have expanded

to fill the time no longer available for it.

Barbara Ehrenreich

But the mother's yearning,

that completest type of the life in another life

which is the essence of real human love,

feels the presence of the cherished child

even in the debased, degraded man.

George Eliot

The lullaby is the spell whereby

the mother attempts to transform herself

back from an ogre to a saint.

James Fenton

You learn that taking care of yourself

is something you do in order to keep yourself alive

so that they can rely on you.

You have to give them a consistent environment

where they can be fed and bathed and clothed

and entertained and educated and loved

and not necessarily in that order.

Carrie Fisher

Once a year, those of us who are already mothers

should tip our hats to the truth.

Ultimately, children don't fit into a schedule.

They expand it, complicate it, enrich it.

In motherhood business, time is still more crucial

than timing, timing, timing.

Ellen Goodman

How many hopes and fears,

how many ardent wishes and anxious apprehensions

are twisted together in the threads

that connect the parent with the child!

Samuel Griswold Goodrich

Only mothers can think of the future—

because they give birth to it in their children.

Maxim Gorky

Children and mothers never truly part—

bound in the beating of each other's heart.

Charlotte Gray

I'd rather be a mother than anyone on earth

Bringing up a child or two of unpretentious birth…

I'd rather tuck a little child all safe and sound in bed

Than twine a chain of diamonds

about my (carefree) head.

I'd rather wash a smudgy face

with round, bright, baby eyes

Than paint the pageantry of fame

or walk among the wise.

Meredith Gray

It was the tiniest thing I ever decided to put

my whole life into.

Terri Guillemets

A woman has two smiles that an angel might envy—

the smile that accepts a lover

before words are uttered, and the smile

that lights on the first born babe,

and assures it of a mother's love.

Thomas C. Haliburton

At every level children are

both creative and the objects of creativity

for they are literally making themselves

and being made at the same time.

Parents are therefore constantly

being re-made as well.

Fraser Harrison

Before you were born I carried you under my heart.

From the moment you arrived in this world

until the moment I leave it,

I will always carry you in my heart.

Mary Harrison

I believe that each personality is

complete at conception

and comes in the soul of every child.

Taylor Hartman

Before you were conceived I wanted you

Before you were born I loved you

Before you were here an hour I would die for you

This is the miracle of Mother's Love.

Maureen Hawkins

The art of mothering

is to teach the art of living to children.

Elaine Heffiner

A mother's arms are made of tenderness

and children sleep soundly in them.

Victor Hugo

The tie which links mother and child

is of such pure and immaculate strength

as to be never violated.

Washington Irving

GOD could not be everywhere.

That's why he made mothers.

Jewish Proverb

Having children makes you no more a parent

than having a piano makes you a pianist.

Michael Levine

When you are a mother,

you are never really alone in your thoughts.

A mother always has to think twice,

once for herself and once for her child.

Sophia Loren

More than in any other human relationship,

overwhelmingly more motherhood means being

instantly interruptible, responsive, responsible.

Tillie Olse

Parents have the glorious opportunity

of being the most powerful influence,

above and beyond any other,

on the new lives that bless their homes.

L. Tom Perry

Every mother is like Moses.

She does not enter the promised land.

She prepares a world she will not see.

Pope Paul VI

Maternity is on the face of it an unsociable experience. The selfishness that a woman has learned to stifle or to dissemble where she alone is concerned, blooms freely and unashamed on behalf of her offspring.

Emily James Putnam

The moment a child is born, the mother is born also.

She never existed before.

The woman existed, but not the mother, never.

A mother is something absolutely new.

Rajneesh

When you wake up one day and say,

"You know what? I don't think I ever need to

sleep or have sex again."

Congratulations, you're ready (to have children).

Ray Romano

To become a mother is one of life's greatest blessings.

It is a lifelong event that forever changes you.

Becoming a mother changes your heart,

your thoughts, and your actions. However,

you may soon wish you had a few extra hands.

Alli Ross

The hand that rocks the cradle

is the hand that rules the world.

W. S. Ross

Parents sometimes think of newborns

as helpless creatures, but in fact parents' behavior

is much more under the infant's control

than the reverse.

Does he come running when you cry?

Sandra Scarr

Children are the anchors that hold a mother to life.

Sophicles

In automobile terms,

the child supplies the power

but the parents have to do the steering.

Benjamin Spock

The more people have studied different methods of

bringing up children the more they have come to the

conclusion that what good mothers and fathers

instinctively feel like doing for their babies

is the best after all.

Benjamin Spock

You see your child as a companion

with the qualities you have or would like to have.

Naemi Stilman, M.D.

Making the decision to have a child is momentous.

It is to decide forever to have your heart

go walking around outside your body.

Elizabeth Stone

Motherhood has a very humanizing effect.

Everything gets reduced to essentials.

Meryl Streep

Being a full-time mother

is one of the highest salaried jobs in my field,

since the payment is pure love.

Mildred B. Vermont

Parents of young children should realize

that few people, and maybe no one,

will find their children as enchanting as they do.

Barbara Walters

INDEX

A
Anonymous, 8-11, 34-36, 64-68
Arabic Proverb, 12
Aristotle, 114
Armor, Joyce, 12, 36
Arms, Suzanne, 37

B
Bacon, Francis, 114
Barry, Dave, 13, 37-39, 69
Beecher, Henry Ward, 115
Berends, Polly B., 115-116
Berle, Milton, 117
Billings, Josh, 69
Bishop, Russell, 70
Blake, William, 39
Blakely, Mary Kay, 40
Bloomingdale, Theresa, 70
Blum, Leon, 117
Bly, David, 118
Bombeck, Erma, 118
Brand, Jo, 41
Brazelton, T. Berry, 71
Broderick, Matthew, 71
Broun, Heywood, 72
Brown, Tina, 72
Buckley, Sarah, 41
Burke, Leo J., 73
Burnett, Carol, 42

C
Carroll, Diahann, 119
Chalmers, Irena, 73
Chinese Proverb, 74, 119-120
Chopra, Deepak, 74
Clark, Frank, 75
Colette, Sidonie Gabrielle, 13
Cosby, Bill, 76

D
Dalton, Nikki, 121
Day, Clarence, 76
Di Orio, Virginia, 42
Dickens, Charles, 77
Dick-Read, Grantly, 43
Diller, Phyllis, 14
Dogen, 121
Dyson, Doris, 78

E
Ehrenreich, Barbara, 15, 122
Eliot, George, 122
Emerson, Ralph Waldo, 78
Ephron, Nora, 79
Erasmus, Desiderius, 43, 79
Erikson, Erik H., 80

F
Fenton, James, 123
Fife, Shannon, 80
Filterman, Linda, 44
Fioretto, Connie, 16
Fischer, Martin H., 44
Fisher, Carrie, 16, 123
Fonda, Jane, 81
Forster, Margaret, 17
Foxworthy, Jeff, 45
Franklin, Benjamin, 17
Freeman, Eileen Elias, 82
Funicello, Annette, 45

G
Gallagher, Robert, 82
Gifford, Kathie Lee, 46
Glaser, Sherry, 46
Goodman, Ellen, 124
Goodrich, Samuel G., 124
Gorky, Maxim, 125
Gray, Charlotte, 125
Gray, Meredith, 126
Greene, Bob, 83
Guillemets, Terri, 127

H
Haliburton, Thomas C., 127
Hall, Barbara, 47
Hamilton, Natasha, 18
Harding, Mike, 83
Harm, Laura Stavoe, 48
Harrison, Fraser, 128
Harrison, Mary, 128
Hartigan, Harriette, 48
Hartman, Taylor, 129
Hatcher, Melissa, 18
Hawkins, Maureen, 129
Heffiner, Elaine, 130
Herold, Don, 19, 84

Hicks, Bill, 49
Hoffenstein, Samuel, 84
Howe, Ed, 85
Hubbard, Kin, 85
Hudson, Kate, 19
Hugo, Victor, 130

I
Irving, Washington, 131
Ivins, Molly, 20

J
Jerome K. Jerome, 86
Jewish Proverb, 131
Jillian, Ann, 86
Johnson, Beverly, 49
Johnstone, Maurice, 87
Jones, Catherine, 20

K
Kennedy, Florence R., 21
Kennedy, Rose Fitzgerald, 87
Kerr, Jean, 88
Key, Ellen, 88
Koch, Liz, 50
Kubic, Peggy, 89
Kutner, Lawrence, 21, 89

L
Lansky, Bruce, 90
Largen, Christopher, 51
Latet, Carrie, 22
Le Shan, Eda J., 90
Leach, Penelope, 91
Leslie, Amy, 91
Levine, Michael, 132
Lim, Robin, 51
Loren, Sophia, 132
Lynn, Loretta, 22

M
MacDonald, George, 92
MacFarlane, Aidan, 52
MacPherson, Elle, 23
Manson, Mary, 92
Marquis, Don, 93
Marsh, Mary, 23
Marzollo, Jean, 24, 52

INDEX

Mason, Ruth, 93
McCarthy, Jenny, 52
McCue, Heather, 54
McLuhan, Marshall, 94
McOmber, Susan, 94
Miller, Henry, 54
Mitchell, Margaret, 55
Montessori, Maria, 95
Morgan, Laurie Annis, 55
Morrison, Andrew P., 95

N
Nash, Ogden, 96
Nathanson, Bernard, 24
Nietzsche, Friedrich, 25
Nolte, Dorothy L., 96

O
O'Donnell, Rosie, 97
Olse, Tillie, 133
Orben, Robert, 97
Osgood, Charles, 98

P
Paul, Robert, 98
Perry, L. Tom, 133
Philips, Emo, 56
Pope Paul VI, 134
Putnam, Emily James, 134

Q
Quindlen, Anna, 56, 99

R
Rajneesh, 135
Reagan, Ronald, 100
Reiser, Paul, 101
Ripley, Fay, 25
Robin, Henry, 102
Roker, Al, 26
Romano, Ray, 135
Romney, Mitt, 26
Roosevelt, Eleanor, 57
Ross, Alli, 136
Ross, W. S., 136
Rothman, Barbara Katz, 58
Rudner, Rita, 27-28
Runyon, Damon, 102
Ryan, Molly, 28

S
Sandburg, Carl, 103
Sarton, May, 103
Scarr, Sandra, 104, 137
Seifert, Barbara Christine, 104
Sexton, Anne, 105
Sexton, Linda Gray, 105
Shire, David, 107
Sikin, Penny, 29
Smith, Elinor Goulding, 107
Sophicles, 137
Spock, Benjamin, 138
Stanislavsky, Constantine, 29
Stavhana, Hla 30
Steinem, Gloria, 58
Steiner-Rice, Helen, 108
Stilman, Naemi, 139
Stilson, Jeff, 59
Stone, Elizabeth, 139
Streep, Meryl, 140

T
Tupper, Martin Fraquhar, 109
Twain, Mark, 109

V
Van Gogh, Vincent, 110
Van Oploo, Anne Marie, 60
Vermont, Mildred B., 140
Vincent, Peggy, 60-61

W
Walters, Barbara, 141
Weideman, Jane, 61
West, Jessamyn, 111
Wiggin, Kate Douglas, 111
Wilson, Robert Anton, 30
Wollstonecraft, Mary, 31
Wordsworth, William, 112

www.ingramcontent.com/pod-product-compliance
Lightning Source LLC
Chambersburg PA
CBHW051806040426
42446CB00007B/538